World Crafts and Recipes

Recipe and Craft Guide to

INDIA

Khadija Ejaz

Mitchell Lane

P.O. Box 196
Hockessin, Delaware 19707
Visit us on the web: www.mitchelllane.com
Comments? email us: mitchelllane@mitchelllane.com

Mitchell Lane
PUBLISHERS

World Crafts and Recipes

The Caribbean • China • France• India • Indonesia • Japan

Copyright © 2011 by Mitchell Lane Publishers

All rights reserved. No part of this book may be reproduced without written permission from the publisher. Printed and bound in the United States of America.

PUBLISHER'S NOTE: The facts on which the story in this book is based have been thoroughly researched. Documentation of such research can be found on page 60. While every possible effort has been made to ensure accuracy, the publisher will not assume liability for damages caused by inaccuracies in the data, and makes no warranty on the accuracy of the information contained herein.

To reflect current usage, we have chosen to use the secular era designations BCE ("before the common era") and CE ("of the common era") instead of the traditional designations BC ("before Christ") and AD (*anno Domini*, "in the year of the Lord").

Library of Congress Cataloging-in-Publication Data

Ejaz, Khadija.
  Recipe and craft guide to India / by Khadija Ejaz.
    p. cm. — (World crafts and recipes)
  Includes bibliographical references and index.
  ISBN 978-1-58415-938-4 (library bound)
  1. Cookery, India—Juvenile literature. 2. Handicraft—India—Juvenile literature. I. Title.
  TX724.5.I4E36 2010
  641.5954—dc22

                                        2010008950

Printing 1 2 3 4 5 6 7 8 9

                                             PLB

CONTENTS

Introduction
Incredible India!

Ay aab-rood-e gangaa! Voh din hain yaad tujhko?
Utraa tere kinaaray jab kaaravaan hamaaraa!
(O the flowing waters of the Ganges, do you remember those days?
When our caravan first disembarked upon your shores!)
—Allama Sir Dr. Muhammad Iqbal, 1877–1938

India as the country we know today is only a little over sixty years old, but its rich history goes back thousands of years. Modern India arose after centuries of intermingling among its original inhabitants and those who migrated to the region from various other parts of the world. India is similar to the United States in this way. Migrant populations from the Middle East, Persia, and Europe greatly influenced the local culture.

India's earliest inhabitants lived in the valley of the Indus River around 2500 BCE. A few hundred years later, Central-Asian nomads called Aryans migrated south past the Himalayas into the fertile plains of the Ganga River, pushing the natives, the Dravidians, farther south. Turkish and Afghani invaders established various kingdoms in North India, the greatest of which evolved into the Mughal Empire, which gave the world the Taj Mahal. After Europe discovered sea routes to India, nations such as Portugal, France, the Netherlands, and Great Britain laid colonial claim to the region. The Indian struggle for independence from the British Empire, which controlled the largest part of India, culminated in the creation of Muslim-dominated Pakistan and Hindu-dominated India on August 14 and 15, 1947, respectively.

As in the Americas, the migrants to India contributed a great deal to the culture of their new home, especially in matters of religion. Hinduism is thought to have evolved from the beliefs of the Aryans; Islam was

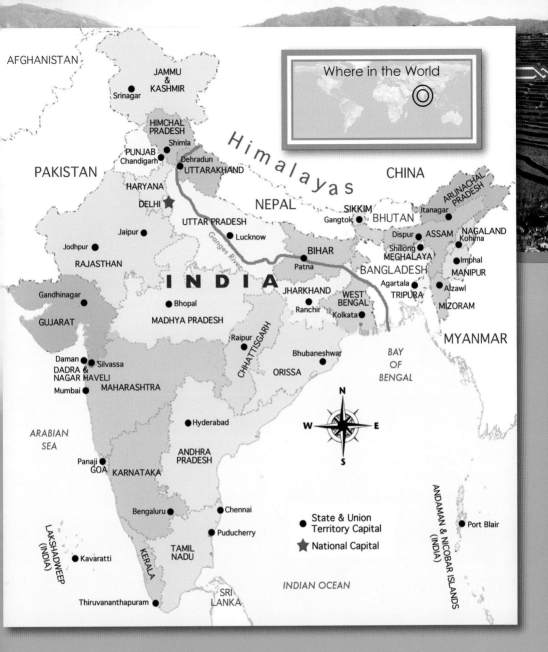

introduced to India by the Arabs, Turks, and Afghanis; Christianity was imported by the Europeans; and Zoroastrianism was brought by the Persians. Over time, the migrants' own foreign customs acquired a distinctive Indian flavor. India's strategic position on the ancient Silk Route also contributed to a tremendous amount of cultural exchange in the region. Today, no region of India is like any other. Tourists are often amazed at how languages, art and music, food, and clothing seem to change every few kilometers.

Here are a few tips to make your time in the kitchen fun and delicious.

Read through the recipe—all the way—before you start. Stopping halfway through the cooking process because you don't have the right ingredients or cookware is a waste of food. Plus, you'll still be hungry!

Wear old clothes and an apron. Wash your hands with warm water and soap before you start.

Be very careful! Always get help from **an adult** when you are using the oven, the stovetop, or sharp knives. Use oven mitts to lift hot baking sheets and pans. Protect the counter with a trivet before you set down a hot container.

Clean up right away. We all know cleaning is the least fun part of cooking, but the sooner you do it, the easier it will be.

Once you've made a recipe successfully, you can experiment the next time. Change the ingredients. Use blueberries instead of raspberries, or honey instead of sugar.

Finally, share your food with your friends and family. Seeing people enjoy your cooking is as much fun as enjoying it yourself!

NOTE: Most of the ingredients used in these recipes can be purchased from your local grocery store. Those available only in Indian specialty stores will be noted.

Nowhere is this diversity reflected more than in the cuisine. In one country, you can find communities that eat beef or don't, eat eggs or don't, eat onions or don't, eat pork or don't, eat any meat or don't. The combinations are endless. Although there are wide variations, no matter what your dietary preferences—whether you eat vegetarian, vegan, or halal food—India will never let you go hungry.

The author of the book reflects India's signature diversity. Khadija Ejaz was born in Lucknow, Uttar Pradesh (UP), in the early hours of an Indian summer day. Her father's paternal side hails from the state of UP, while his maternal side originates from the Pathan communities of present-day Afghanistan and the North-West Frontier Province of modern Pakistan. Khadija's mother was born to the Ansari family of Lucknow, who trace

their lineage back to the Ansars of Medina, Saudi Arabia. Ansar ("helper" in Arabic) was the name given to the tribes who welcomed the Prophet Mohammed (peace be upon him) into their city in 622 CE. In Lucknow, the Ansari family founded the Muslim religious school of Firangi Mahal, which played a pivotal role in the evolution of Islam in India from the seventeenth to the twentieth centuries. The estate that housed the school was presented to the Ansaris by the Mughal emperor Aurangzeb.

Indians may or may not eat meat; they may worship Bhagwan, Allah, Ahura Mazda, God, Yahweh, or Waheguru; they may even look typically Indian, East Asian, European, or Middle Eastern. That is the magical embrace of Mother India. No matter whether you come from over the great Himalayas in the north or from across the three great seas in the south, once you arrive, you'll know India was always home.

> *Gar firdaus bar rooh-e-zameen ast, hameen ast, hameen ast, hameen ast.*
> (If there is a paradise on Earth, it is here, it is here, it is here.)
> —Mughal Emperor Nur-ud-din Salim Jahangir, 1569–1627

Paapad

Can you champion this famous Hindi tongue twister—*kachchaa paapad, pakkaa paapad* (raw *paapad*, cooked *paapad*)? These thin crispy wafers are made of lentils, chickpeas, black grams, rice flour, or potatoes, and can be eaten as a snack or as an appetizer. Maybe you've come across them by their popular name, *papadums*. These crunchy "chips" come in all sizes but are mostly round. *Paapad* can be fried, roasted, or even microwaved and eaten with various toppings and dips.

Ingredients:

4 cups lentil flour (available at your local Indian grocery store)
½ teaspoon cracked black pepper
½ teaspoon ground cumin seeds
¼ teaspoon salt
⅛ cup water
Cooking oil
1 small red onion, finely chopped
1 green chili, finely chopped
Lemon juice, to taste

Instructions:

1. Mix flour, pepper, cumin, and salt.
2. Add water and knead the dough until it is smooth.
3. Add more water if the dough seems too dry.
4. Split the dough into 5 or 7 balls. On a slightly oiled surface, roll them out one ball at a time into a very thin circle.
5. Place the *paapads* on a cookie sheet and dry them in a warm oven (about 200°F) for an hour.
6. In a large frying pan, add enough cooking oil to completely submerge the *paapad,* and set it to high heat. To test if the oil is

ready, **ask an adult** to drop a tiny piece of *paapad* in it. If the *paapad* begins to cook immediately, turn the heat to medium.

7. **Ask an adult** to submerge the whole paapad in the oil and fry it. The *paapad* should begin to cook immediately. Turn it over once. Take it out quickly before it begins to brown.

8. Place the cooked *paapad* on a plate lined with a paper towel to absorb any excess oil.

9. Repeat with the other *paapad* or place the extra ones in an airtight container to use later.

10. Sprinkle the onion, chilies, and lemon juice on the cooked *paapad*. Serve immediately.

FUN FACT: Black grams are black lentils that originated in India and are highly prized there. In a funny twist, they are sometimes called white lentils. The white lentils are the same bean; they simply have the black coat removed.

Dhokla

Dhokla, a spongy appetizer, is a specialty from Gujarat in western India—the state that gave India the freedom fighter Mohandas Karamchand Gandhi. Traditionally, *dhokla* is made by steaming a fermented batter of gram flour, a popular ingredient that is available in any Indian grocery store. Gram flour, also known as *besan,* is made from chickpeas. Once steamed, the *dhokla* is cut into pieces and tempered with a dressing of fried mustard seeds and cumin. Don't forget the chutney with this quick microwavable version of the popular Indian snack!

Ingredients:

For the *dhokla:*
½ cup gram flour (available at your local Indian grocery store)
¼ cup cooking oil
½ teaspoon salt
½ cup water
1 teaspoon baking powder
   Coriander, finely chopped
   Green chilies, finely chopped

For the tempering:
1 tablespoon cooking oil
1 teaspoon mustard
½ teaspoon cumin

Instructions:

To prepare the *dhokla:*
1. In a bowl, add the gram flour, oil, and salt. Mix well.
2. Add the baking powder to the water and mix well. Immediately add to the gram flour mixture. Stir until smooth.
3. Pour into a microwavable dish that's been greased with oil or butter.
4. Microwave the mixture uncovered for 3 minutes or until a toothpick inserted into the *dhokla* comes out clean.

5. After the *dhokla* has cooled, cut it into large squares and arrange them on a plate.

Under adult supervision, prepare the tempering:
1. In a frying pan, heat the oil on high.
2. Add the mustard and cumin to the oil. Watch out for splatters!
3. Sauté the mustard and cumin until the cumin begins to brown, then quickly remove the pan from the stove and pour the mixture over the *dhokla*.
4. Garnish the *dhokla* with the coriander and green chilies. Serve with chutney.

FUN FACT: Chutney is a kind of Indian dipping sauce, similar to salsa, marinara, hummus, and even ketchup. Different kinds of chutney can be purchased at your local Indian grocery store or made fresh at home.

Mach Bhaja

In eastern India lies the state of West Bengal, home to the proud Bengalis (what used to be East Bengal is now part of the country of modern-day Bangladesh). Rabindranath Tagore, Asia's first Nobel laureate and the composer of the national anthems of India and Bangladesh, was from Calcutta, the capital of West Bengal. Maybe the region's proximity to the Ganga and Brahmaputra rivers and the Bay of Bengal is the reason the Bengalis include a lot of fish in their diet of lentils and rice. Enjoy this fried (*bhaja*) fish (*mach*) the Bengali way or on its own as a delicious snack.

Ingredients:

1 pound fish filets, such as cod or haddock
1 tablespoon ginger paste
1 tablespoon garlic paste
  Salt, to taste
¼ teaspoon ground black pepper
2 tablespoons lemon juice
2 eggs
½ cup pastry flour
1 cup bread crumbs
  Cooking oil, to deep-fry

Instructions:

1. Wash fish filets and cut them into half-inch thick strips. Wash them again under running water. Pat them dry and arrange them in a deep-sided dish that can be covered.
2. Mix together ginger paste, garlic paste, salt, black pepper, and lemon juice. Pour the mixture over the fish. Cover and put in the refrigerator overnight.
3. Beat the eggs in a shallow bowl.

4. Pour the flour in a second shallow bowl, and the breadcrumbs in a third shallow bowl.
5. Coat the fish strips with flour. Rub off any the extra flour, then roll them roll in the eggs, and finally in the breadcrumbs.
6. **Under adult supervision,** heat enough oil in a wok to deep-fry the fish. Cook until golden brown.
7. Using tongs, place the fish on a plate lined with paper towels to drain excess oil. Serve hot.

FUN FACT: In India, this dish would be made with *maida* instead of pastry flour. *Maida* is finely milled, like pastry flour, and is used in many Indian baked goods, including pastries, bread, and biscuits.

Chicken *Karhai*

Aptly named after the iron wok in which it is prepared, *karhai* (wok) chicken is a favorite Mughlai (Mughal) dish from North India. Typical Mughlai cuisine combines meat such as lamb, chicken, or beef with aromatic spices in the tradition of the Persian and Turkic people from Central Asia. Enjoy this mouthwatering dish, a royal legacy of the Mughal Empire, together with any Indian bread.

Ingredients:

½ cup cooking oil
1 medium onion, chopped
2 cloves
2 cardamoms
1 chicken, cut into pieces
1 tablespoon plain yogurt
3 tablespoons ginger paste
3 tablespoons garlic paste
2 teaspoons salt
6 medium tomatoes, chopped
8 green chilies, whole with top cut off
   Coriander, chopped
   Ginger, chopped

Instructions:

Make this recipe under adult supervision.
1. In a wok, heat the oil on high.
2. Add the onions, cloves, and cardamoms to the oil. Cook until the onions lose their color and begin to brown.

3. Turn the heat to low. Add the chicken, yogurt, ginger, garlic, and salt to the oil. Watch out for splatters!
4. Turn the heat to high and cook until the oil begins to separate.
5. Add the tomatoes and 6 green chilies. Cook covered on medium heat until the chicken is cooked thoroughly and a light sauce remains.
6. Garnish with chopped coriander and ginger and the remaining green chilies.

Aaloo Matar Tamaatar

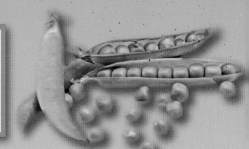

No collection of Indian recipes would be complete without a vegetarian dish. Millions of Hindus are strictly vegetarian; some do not even eat eggs. This recipe for *aaloo matar tamaatar* (potatoes peas tomatoes) can be used to prepare other light yet buttery vegetarian dishes. It goes well with Indian bread, pickles, lentils, and rice.

Ingredients:

4 tablespoons oil
1 medium red onion, chopped
2 cloves
2 cardamoms
2 medium tomatoes, chopped
1 tablespoon ginger paste
1 tablespoon garlic paste
1 tablespoon onion paste
½ teaspoon coriander powder
¾ teaspoon red chili powder
2 medium potatoes, chopped
2 cups peas
3 teaspoons salt
2 cups water
Coriander, finely chopped

Instructions:

Make this recipe under adult supervision.
1. In an uncovered pot, heat the oil on high.
2. Before the oil heats up too much, add the onion, cloves, and cardamoms to it. Watch out for splatters!
3. When the onion loses its color and begins to brown, add the tomatoes, ginger paste, garlic paste, onion paste, coriander powder, and red chili powder to the pot.

4. When the oil begins to separate from the spice mixture, add the potatoes. Cook covered on low heat for 5 minutes.
5. Add the peas, salt, and water.
6. Bring the water to a boil.
7. Let the vegetables simmer on medium heat until the potatoes are thoroughly cooked. They are done when they are soft and easy to break. Keep enough water in the pot to create a light sauce.
8. Garnish with chopped coriander.

FUN FACT: Followers of the Jain faith do not eat anything that will harm another organism, including plants. For this reason, they are vegetarians, and they also do not eat vegetables that grow in the ground, such as onions, carrots, and potatoes.

Chanay (Chickpeas)

Vegetarians do not miss out on protein—they get it from beans, vegetables, and other sources. This preparation of *chanay* (chickpeas) hails from the northern state of Punjab and can be eaten on its own, with Indian bread, or in combination with a *chaat* (Indian snack) platter.

Ingredients:

½ teaspoon baking powder
2 cups water
1 cup chickpeas
4 tablespoons oil
½ teaspoon cumin
1 medium tomato, chopped
1½ teaspoons salt
½ teaspoon red chili powder
  Coriander, finely chopped
  Onions, finely chopped
  Ginger, finely chopped
  Green chilies, finely chopped
  Lemon juice, to taste

Instructions:

Make this recipe under adult supervision.
1. In a bowl, dissolve the baking powder in the water.
2. Soak the chickpeas in the water overnight.
3. The next day, drain the water from the chickpeas but don't throw it out.
4. In a pressure cooker, heat the oil with the cumin on high until the cumin begins to brown. If you don't have a pressure cooker, you can use a regular pot instead and adjust the cooking time to about two hours. Just be sure there is plenty of water in the pot and that the chickpeas are done (see step 11).
5. Turn the heat to low.

6. Add the chickpeas, tomato, salt, and red chili powder to the pressure cooker. Watch out for splatter!
7. Add the soaking water to half an inch above the settled chickpeas.
8. Close the lid of the cooker. Turn the heat to high.
9. After the first whistle, turn the heat to low for 20 minutes.
10. Turn off the heat for 15 minutes.
11. When the gas has escaped the cooker, open the lid and check the chickpeas. They should be soft but still retain their shape. If not, then let them simmer on low until they are finished cooking.
12. Simmer until a light sauce remains.
13. Garnish with coriander, onions, ginger, and green chilies. Sprinkle with lemon juice.

Matar Chaawal

Add some excitement and color to plain boiled rice *(chaawal)* by adding peas *(matar)* to it. You may even substitute any other vegetable, or combination of vegetables, for the peas. This dish is good with pickles and plain yogurt, but it is nutritious enough to eat on its own. It's great when you're in the mood for something light, or to change the taste and texture of other meat or vegetarian dishes.

Ingredients:

- 1 cup rice
- 3 tablespoons cooking oil
- 4 cloves
- 4 cardamoms
- 1 bay leaf
- 1 cinnamon stick
- 2 cups peas
- 2 teaspoons salt
- 2 green chilies, chopped
- 1 tablespoon ginger paste
- ½ teaspoon cumin

Make this recipe under adult supervision.

1. Wash the rice. Cover it with water that is an inch higher than the settled rice.
2. In a pot, heat the oil on high.
3. Add the cumin, cloves, cardamoms, bay leaf, and cinnamon sticks to the oil and brown them.
4. Add the peas, salt, green chilies, and ginger paste to the oil. Watch out for splatters! Cook until you can smell the peas.
5. Add the rice and soaking water to the pot. Bring to a boil.
6. Turn the heat down to low. Cook until the rice has puffed without losing its shape. Test the rice by pressing one piece between your fingers; it should be firm but not crunchy or soft.
7. Evaporate excess water.

Payasam

Payasam is a signature milk-based South Indian dessert. An integral part of South Indian culture, this dish is also known by various other names all over the country, including *payesh* in West Bengal and *sivaiyn* in the Hindi- and Urdu-speaking communities. In a nation where sweet dishes accompany any joyous celebration, *payasam* is most often prepared to mark special occasions such as festivals and other happy events.

Ingredients:

8-10 almonds
8-10 pistachios
Saffron, a few strands (optional; available
   at your local Indian grocery store)
2 quarts cream
2 tablespoons ghee (clarified butter)
   (available at your local Indian grocery store)
4 ounces vermicelli
8-10 raisins
¼ teaspoon cardamom powder
½ cup sugar

Instructions:

Make this recipe under adult supervision.
1. Blanch the almonds and the pistachios.
2. Drain, peel, and cut the almonds and pistachios into slivers.
3. Soak the saffron in 2 tablespoons of warm milk.
4. In a thick-bottomed vessel, heat the rest of the milk on high heat and bring to a boil. Reduce the heat and let the milk simmer, stirring continuously until it is thick and reduced to half the original quantity. Be careful that the milk doesn't boil over.

To blanch nuts, cover them with boiling water and let them sit for 1 minute (almonds) or 2 minutes (shelled pistachios). Have an adult drain them, and let them cool. Rub them gently to remove the thin outer skin.

5. In a frying pan, heat the ghee on high. When the ghee is hot, reduce the heat to low and add the vermicelli. Brown it for 3-4 minutes or until light golden. Be careful, vermicelli burns quickly!
6. Add the vermicelli to the milk in the pot. Heat the milk on high and bring it to a boil again.
7. Reduce heat to low and let it simmer for 2-3 minutes.
8. Add the saffron, almonds, pistachios, raisins, cardamom powder, and sugar to the milk. Continue to simmer for another 5 minutes.
9. Serve hot.

Besan ke Laddoo

It is practically impossible to think of any Indian festival or celebration without *laddoos*. These ubiquitous yellow balls are made of ghee and sugar, two ingredients that signify happiness and prosperity in India. *"Tumhaare moonh mein ghee shakar"* (May your mouth be full of ghee and sugar) is a common Hindi expression used to bless the bearer of good news. A beloved and well-fed child is also sometimes affectionately called a *laddoo*.

Ingredients:

½ cup ghee
1 cup gram flour
   (available at your local
   Indian grocery store)
¾ cup superfine sugar

Instructions:

1. In a frying pan, heat the ghee on medium heat.
2. Add the gram flour to the oil and keep stirring until the gram flour begins to turn light brown.
3. Immediately pour the gram flour into a mixing bowl.
4. After the mixture has cooled, add the sugar to the gram flour. Mix well.
5. Use your hands to make *laddoos* in the shape of balls. Keep them firm by applying pressure with your hands.
6. Let the *laddoos* cool before serving. They will need to harden a bit before they can be eaten.

Sharbat

Made popular in India by the Mughals, a *sharbat* is a chilled sweet drink made of fruits and flowers. The words *sherbet* (English), *sorbet* (French), and *sorbetto* (Italian) are all derived from *sharbat*, the Arabic word for "drink." The most popular ingredient in *sharbats* is Rooh Afza, a syrup made from the essence of rose petals. Rooh Afza drinks are popular in the summer and during Ramadan, the Muslim month of fasting. The name Rooh Afza is Urdu for something that elevates the soul.

Ingredients:

1 cup water or milk
3 tablespoons Rooh Afza syrup
(available at your local Indian grocery
store)
Ice cubes
Lemon juice, to taste

Instructions:

1. Add the Rooh Afza to the water or milk and
   stir until the syrup has dissolved completely.
2. Add the ice cubes and lemon juice.
3. Drink cold.

India Crafts

Indian art can be best understood if viewed within its cultural, historical, religious, and philosophical context. To gain a deeper insight into the inspiration and meaning behind a given form of art, one will have to locate its position on India's cultural timeline. Most Indian art can be broadly classified within at least one of the following periods:

- Ancient period (3500 BCE–1200 CE)
- Islamic ascendency (712 CE–1757 CE)
- European colonial period (1757 CE–1947 CE)
- Independence and the postcolonial period (post-1947 CE)

Indian culture is heavily derived from its religious traditions. The Hindus, Buddhists, and Jains gave form to their deities and their mythologies in sculptures and paintings. The magnificent rock sculptures at the Ajanta, Ellora, and Elephanta caves are a good example of Indian religious beliefs manifesting themselves through

art. Because Islam discourages the artistic representation of living beings, the Muslims developed specialized metalwork, pottery, painting, fabric, carpet, and calligraphy skills. The Muslims also made distinctive contributions to the fields of architecture. The Taj Mahal in Agra, a Mughal creation and one of the seven wonders of the modern world, is one such legacy of Islam in India. Similarly, Sikhism, Christianity, Zoroastrianism, Judaism, and other tribal beliefs have influenced Indian art on many levels.

The craft projects included in this book are only your first steps into the everyday Indian cultural scene. You can build on these ideas to come up with more complex projects. Most of the materials needed to complete the projects in this book can be easily obtained from various sources, such as in your house (even your kitchen!), in nature, and in craft stores. If you keep your work colorful and bright, you cannot go wrong. Get creative with the tip of this iceberg—like India, art is forever evolving.

Cool Secrets for Creating Great Crafts

Read through the instructions—all the way—before you start. This tip can be hard to follow, because you might be so eager to start, you'll dive right in. That's the right spirit! But read all the way through anyway. You'll be glad you did.

Gather all your materials first. A missing item might make you stop halfway through, and then you won't feel like finishing.

Protect your work surface. Lay down newspaper or a plastic tablecloth. (This is a step your parents will be glad you took!) Wear old clothes.

Be creative. You might think of a great new step to add or a twist that gives the craft your personal touch. While you're at it, learn from your mistakes. Try a craft a few times to get it right. Your craft doesn't have to look like the one in the picture to be great.

Be careful. When the instructions tell you to get help from an adult, you know what you should do? You guessed it. Get help from an adult!

Clean up right away. It's much easier to clean paintbrushes, wipe down surfaces, and wash tools (including your hands) while the mess is fresh. Plus, when you ask for permission to start a new project, you can remind your parents that you cleaned up last time. You could also ask your parents to join you. Crafts are even more fun when someone does them with you.

As you go about your everyday activities, save things that might be good for your projects. Shoeboxes, toilet paper rolls, ribbon and tissue paper from a gift—these can all be used to make crafts that you'll enjoy keeping or giving to friends and family.

The final secret? Have fun! If you don't enjoy it, there's no point in crafting.

Flower Garland

Life in India is bright, exploding with color, exploding with life. Black, brown, gray, and white express the opposite of all that is happy and are used only during times of mourning and grief. Flowers, therefore, are used for their beautiful shades and fragrances to mark any auspicious occasion. You'd be hard-pressed to find an Indian celebration that isn't embellished with flowers, especially strung up with garlands. Flower garlands are used during weddings and for welcoming guests. Before sending one of their own off on a long journey, a family will bless and offer luck to their loved one with a garland. Some Hindu families even drape a fresh garland around the picture of a deceased family member.

Materials:

Thread
Scissors
Measuring tape
Needle
Crepe paper, any color
Pencil

Instructions:

1. Cut off a 30-inch-long piece of thread. Two inches from one end, tie a double knot and thread the needle with the other end.
2. Cut off a 2.5-inch-wide section of crepe paper from one end of the folded packet.
3. On the cut-off section of paper, draw three lines lengthwise to divide the paper into equal thirds.
4. Make a number of cuts into both the long edges of the cut-off section, not going past the lines you drew. The cuts on both sides of the paper, therefore, will not be longer than one-third the width of the paper. Make sure to keep half an inch between cuts.

33

5. Unfold the section of paper to get a long strip with cuts into the long edges.

6. Pierce the needle into the paper at one end of the strip and gently draw the thread through the hole until the knot is firmly in place against the paper.

7. Use your needle to make short running stitches in the middle of the strip through the entire length of the strip. Carefully draw the thread through the stitches, pushing the stitched strip down to the bottom of the thread while turning the strip in a spiral fashion. Press the folded strip tightly.

8. Repeat steps 2-7 until a couple of inches remain on the thread. Tie the free end of the thread tightly to the knotted end.

Additional Suggestions:
1. Use different color combinations in your garland.
2. Vary the length of the thread to make garlands of different lengths. You can even make bracelets, anklets, and other ornaments.
3. Make the strips as wide or as long as you like. The width will determine the size of the flowers in the garland. The length and number of strips will determine how much of that color will be incorporated into the garland.

Block Print

Block printing is one of the many handicrafts for which India is known. The beautiful designs are made by pressing painted carved blocks of wood on fabric—similar to how children today make fun ink designs using store-bought rubber stamps. The city of Surat in Gujarat was famous for its printed designs as early as in the twelfth century CE, but the art is still widely practiced all across India.

Materials:

Old newspaper
Cotton shirt, any color
Potatoes of various sizes
Pencil
Sharp knife
Paper towels
Fabric paints, various colors
Paintbrush

Instructions:

1. Cover a flat surface with newspaper. Lay the cotton shirt on it.
2. With **an adult**, cut the potatoes in half.
3. Draw a design with the pencil onto the flat, exposed side of the potato halves.
4. Under **adult supervision,** use the knife to carve the penciled design deep into the potato.
5. Dry the potato with a paper towel.
6. Brush paint onto the carved side of the potato.
7. Press the carved side of the potato onto the shirt. You may want to practice on paper first.
8. Lift the potato from the shirt to see the design you just made.
9. Repeat steps 6-8 until you've completed the block print design. Let the paint dry for at least a day before you show off your new shirt!

Additional Suggestions:

1. You can use potatoes of various sizes, and can even cut them into different shapes before carving them.
2. You can make designs of any color on cloth of any color.
3. You will need to periodically wipe out the accumulated paint from the carved grooves in the potato. This will help prevent your design from becoming blotchy and smudged.
4. Using this technique, you can create beautiful block prints on any clothing items, bedsheets, tablecloths, and even curtains! Just be sure to get permission from your parents first.

Henna

In India, bridal makeup is never complete without the most beautiful and detailed of henna designs. But one doesn't have to be a bride to apply henna to the arms and legs. These reddish brown designs are created by applying the paste derived from the crushed leaves of the henna plant. Some people call these designs tattoos, but they are actually temporary, lasting only from a week to a few months. Also called *mehndi,* henna has cooling properties and is an excellent hair conditioner. If the right substances are added to it, henna can also be used as a hair dye. The boys needn't feel left out; they too can create safe and temporary designs on themselves!

Materials:

Old clothes
Old newspapers
Henna powder
Water
Any bowl
Paintbrush
Cotton balls
Lemon juice

Instructions:

1. Wear old clothes to do this project, as the henna may stain them. You might also want to lay old newspapers on the table where you are working.
2. Mix the henna powder with enough water to make a yogurt-like paste.
3. Dip the paintbrush in the henna paste and use it to carefully create a design on your skin.
4. Using cotton balls, gently apply lemon juice on the henna paste as it dries on your skin. This will help bring out the color of the tattoo. Make sure you don't smudge your design or smear it on your clothes!
5. When your design has completely dried, dust the dried henna paste from your skin. Do not use water or soap on the area for 24 hours.

Doli

Before the people of India used cars and the railway, and even before the time of animal-driven carts, people moved about in palanquins called *dolis* or *palkis*. These vehicles were like covered chairs or beds. They were raised on bamboo poles by palanquin-bearers, who would do the walking. Traditionally available only to the upper crust of society and others who could afford it, palanquins were a luxury, like the modern-day limo. They were most commonly used to transport brides from their parents' homes to their husbands'. That is what they are still nostalgically used for today.

Materials:

Shoebox with a lid
Colored paper
Scissors
Chopsticks
Clear tape
Colorful lace, sequins, etc.
Paint
Glue

Instructions:

1. Remove the lid from the shoebox, keeping it right-side up. The lid will be used as the base of the *doli.*
2. Cover the outsides of the shoebox and lid with the colored paper.
3. Turn the shoebox upside down. This will form the main part of the *doli.*
4. Cut decorative doors on both long sides of the shoebox.
5. Punch holes on both the short sides near the top of the shoebox.
6. Push chopsticks through the holes, keeping a few inches sticking out on both sides. If a chopstick isn't long enough, use more than one and tape them together inside the shoebox.
7. Keeping the lid right-side up, glue the upside down shoebox (with the open end on the bottom) into the lid.
8. Decorate the *doli* with colorful lace and sequins. Wrap the exposed chopsticks with lace and glue the ends to secure it.

Punkha (Fan)

A *punkha* is a fan, and Indians began using handheld ones long before the advent of electricity. Indian summers can get really hot, and are similar to those in countries in the Far East and even in Europe. These small fans provided relief from the high temperatures. Some fans are made of strips of bamboo woven together. Some rotate around a handle. All are decorated with colorful fabric. Large ones were fitted in the homes of the wealthy, where designated servants would fan their owners.

Materials:

Stiff card stock, various colors
Scissors
Ruler
Chopsticks
Shiny lace
Glue
Colorful thick string, lace, or ribbon
Glitter, crayons, stickers, etc.
Paints
Pencil

Instructions:

1. On a large square or rectangular piece of card stock, cut pretty zigzags or curves along three of the edges.
2. Cut another piece of different colored card paper in the same shape as the previous paper, except smaller. Both cutouts will have one straight edge.
3. Glue the smaller cutout onto the larger cutout, keeping the straight edges together. The shorter edge should be placed along the middle of the longer edge.
4. Cut 3 equidistant holes along the straight edge of the fan about half an inch from the edge.
5. Lay two chopsticks along the straight edge of the fan. Adjust the length of the chopsticks according to the size of the fan. The

sticks should protrude an inch or two at the top of the edge, and six inches or so below the edge. This longer part will form the handle.

6. Bind the sticks together by completely wrapping them with shiny lace. Secure the lace by gluing it at the ends of the sticks. Decorate the stick.

7. Position the stick with the straight edge of the fan. Bind the stick to the fan three times with thick string, lace, or ribbon woven through the holes on the fan.

8. Decorate the surface of the fan.

Chakri (Pinwheel)

Life in India has always been about simple pleasures: a refreshing cup of tea, the first raindrops of the monsoon, the *malaai* (cream) off the top of fresh milk. This outlook on life is also found in the children of India who can derive many hours of delight from the simplest toys. The *chakri* (pinwheel) is just one of the many playthings that are familiar to every child living between the northern Himalayas and the southern coast on the Indian Ocean.

Materials:

Craft paper, any color
Scissors
Thumbtack
Pencil with eraser
Colorful lace
Glue

Instructions:

1. Cut out a square piece of any size from the craft paper.
2. Fold the square piece diagonally twice.
3. Unfold the paper to find two intersecting diagonal lines.
4. From all four corners of the square, cut halfway along the diagonals.
5. Without creasing, fold each corner to the center of the square. Pierce a thumbtack through the folded corners and the center of the paper.
6. Poke the end of the thumbtack into the eraser of the pencil.
7. Wrap colorful lace around the pencil, and glue the ends to keep it secure.

Sehra (Headdress)

A *sehra* is a wedding headdress worn by both the bride and groom. It has strands of flowers that dangle over their faces. This veil of flowers is usually drawn to the side as the wedding ceremony is about to begin. Depending on where you are in India, the style of the *sehra* will vary. Some *sehras* are sparse, and you can always see the face of the bride and the groom. Others hide the entire face. Some are short and extend only to the middle of the chest, and some go all the way to the feet! Red roses and white jasmines are most commonly used in *sehras*. They have long-lasting sweet fragrances, and their bright colors seem to sparkle when used with silver and gold threads.

Materials:

Wide piece of colorful lace
Wide piece of colorful ribbon
Thread
Needle
Scissors
Crepe paper, preferably white and red
Ruler
Pencil
Heavy string, preferably gold and silver

Instructions:

1. Wrap a piece of colorful lace around your head like a sweatband. Cut it just a bit shorter than this length. Do the same for a colorful piece of ribbon.
2. Thread the needle and tie a knot at one end.
3. Sew the colorful lace on top of the colorful ribbon with simple running stitches. This will form the headband part of the *sehra.*
4. Cut two 6-inch-long pieces of heavy string. Sew one to each short end of the headband. These will be used to fasten the *sehra* to your head.

47

5. Cut off a 12-inch-long piece of thread. Tie a double knot at one end and thread the needle with the other end.

6. Using wedding colors, follow the instructions for making a flower garland on page 32. This will form the flowers of the *sehra.* Make several of these garlands. There should be enough flower garlands to dangle in front of and fully cover your face.

7. Sew the garlands into the lower long edge of the headband. Try to keep the garlands next to each other, with minimum space between any two pieces. Be sure to knot the threads well.

8. Cut a few pieces of heavy string the same length as the flower garlands. Sew them into the lower long edge of the headband between the flower lengths.

Additional Suggestions:
1. You can vary the length of the flower garlands to make *sehras* of different lengths.
2. You can make the flowers as wide as you like or of any color you like. Each garland is usually made of white flowers with a bunch of red flowers at the bottom. The width of the crepe paper strips will determine the size of the flowers in the garland. The length and number of strips will determine how much of that color will be incorporated into the *sehra*.

Rangoli

Rangoli is a traditional Indian art form that uses colored sand and flower petals. Colored rice flour was originally used to make the designs. The word *Rangoli* is derived from *Rangavalli*, which in turn is made up of the words *rang* (color) and *aavalli* (rows of colors). Another name for this art is Kolam. The designs are used to decorate the floor, doorstep, or walls of one's house or place of worship. The patterns are usually geometrical and can get quite complicated and large, covering whole floors.

You can make a Rangoli design on a large piece of cardboard. If you want to try it on a floor of your home, be sure to get permission first.

Materials:

Large piece of heavy cardboard (optional)
Colored markers or chalk
Rangoli design
Mixing bowls
Food coloring, various colors
Raw rice grains
Salt
Baking sheet
Aluminum foil
Glue (optional)
Raw pulses and grains, various colors
Dried flower petals, various colors
Colored sand

Instructions:

1. On a large piece of cardboard, draw the Rangoli design you would like to make. Typical designs are geometrical or floral. Search for examples on the Internet, or use the one shown on page 53. Color the design with markers. If you have your parents' permission, you may use chalk to draw your design on the driveway or sidewalk, or on a floor, instead of on cardboard.

2. If you want to use rice in your design, then dye the rice with food coloring. Try various colors. In a bowl, evenly mix the rice with a few drops of food coloring. Spread the rice out onto a baking sheet covered with foil, and let it dry.
3. If you want to use salt in your design, then dye the salt the same way you would the rice (see step 2).
4. Apply a thin layer of glue on the cardboard. (DO NOT use glue if your design is on the ground.)
5. Fill the design completely with the colored rice, pulses and grains, flower petals, colored sand, and colored salt. Be careful not to let the colors blend together.

Raakhi

Bhaiyya mere, raakhi ke bandhan ko nibhana . . .
(Brother of mine, remember to keep the promise
of the bond of the *raakhi . . .*)

So goes the song of the 1959 Bollywood movie *Chhoti Behen* (Younger Sister). Raksha Bandhan (the bond of protection) is the Hindu and Sikh festival that celebrates the sacred relationship between a brother and a sister. On this day, sisters tie holy threads or decorative bracelets called *raakhis* on the wrists of their brothers. The brothers give them presents and renew their vow to protect their sisters, and brothers and sisters feed each other sweets. The symbolism of tying a *raakhi* is so powerful and honorable for Indians, Hindu or not, that it can make brothers out of non-brothers—an adopted brother, if you will. The *raakhi*, once tied, is never taken off and stays on the brother's wrist until it falls off completely.

Materials:

Thread
Needle
Scissors
Shiny lace
Shiny string
Gems, sequins, glitter, etc.
Glue
Stapler

FUN FACT: Bollywood is the Indian Hindi film industry, which is based in Mumbai, the capital of the Indian state of Maharashtra. The term comes from *Bombay* (the former name for Mumbai) and *Hollywood*.

Instructions:

1. Thread the needle and tie a knot at one end.
2. Make short running stitches along the undecorated long side of the shiny lace.
3. Firmly push the entire length of lace down the thread against the knotted end until the lace bunches up.
4. Stitch and tie both short ends of the lace together to form a complete circle. Make sure there is no hole in the middle of the circle.
5. Stretch the shiny string out, and place the stitched lace circle in the middle of it. Staple or sew the lace to the string.
6. Decorate the *raakhi* with gems, sequins, glitter, and anything else you feel like. You may use glue or a needle and thread. The brighter the decoration, the better!

Diya

The poet Valmiki narrates the story of the noble king Rama of Ayodhya in his epic poem Ramayana. Some Hindus worship Rama as a deity. They celebrate his return to his kingdom with his brother Lakshmana after rescuing his wife, Sita, from Ravana, the evil king of Lanka. The original occupants of Ayodhya decorated the kingdom with clay oil lamps, or *diyas*, to mark the joyous return of their king after fourteen years of exile. This festival is called Diwali. It is still celebrated in India in the same way that the subjects of Ayodhya once did—by lighting *diyas* in their homes.

Materials:

Small clay pot, such as
    one from a garden center
Paints
Glue
Decorative gems
Little mirrors
Tealight
Matches (and an adult to light them)

Instructions:

1. Paint a bright design on your pot.
2. Decorate it by gluing on gems and little mirrors if you want.
3. When the pot is dry, place the tealight inside it.
4. **Have an adult** light the tealight, then put the *diya* in a safe place.

Further Reading

Books

Dalal, Tarla. *Fun Food for Children.* Mumbia: Sanjay & Co., 2007.

Ejaz, Khadija. *How'd They Do That in the Persian Empire?* Hockessin, Delaware: Mitchell Lane Publishers, 2010.

———. *Meet Our New Student from India.* Hockessin, Delaware: Mitchell Lane Publishers, 2010.

Ganeri, Anita. *A World of Food: India.* Minneapolis, Minnesota: Clara House Books, 2010.

Goulding, Sylvia. *Festive Foods India.* New York: Chelsea Clubhouse, 2008.

Hardyman, Robyn. *Celebrate! India.* New York: Chelsea House Publications, 2009.

Ram-Prasad, Chakravarthi. *Civilizations of the World: Exploring the Life, Myth, and Art of India.* New York: Rosen Publishing Group, 2009.

Works Consulted

This book is based on the author's knowledge and experiences as an Indian in addition to help from her mother, Urdu writer and poet Farzana Ejaz. The author was born in Lucknow, India, and raised in Muscat, Sultanate of Oman. Other sources she used are listed below.

CIA: *The World Factbook,* "India"
https://www.cia.gov/library/publications/the-world-factbook/geos/in.html

Dhamija, Jasleen, and Jyotindra Jain. *Handwoven Fabrics of India.* Ahmedabad, India: Mapin Publishing Pvt. Ltd., 1989.

Guha, Supriya. *A Journey Through India.* New Delhi: Lustre Press Pvt. Ltd., 1990.

Jain, Jyotindra, and Aarti Aggarwala. *National Handicrafts and Handlooms Museum, New Delhi.* Ahmedabad, India: Mapin Publishing Pvt. Ltd., 1989.

Massey, Reginald, Marc Alexander, Kailash Budhwar, Balraj Khanna, Biman Mullick, Swraj Paul, Eilean Pearcey, and Meera Taneja. *All India.* London: Apple Press Ltd., 1986.

Further Reading

Murphy, Veronica, and Rosemary Gill. *Tie-Dyed Textiles of India.* Ahmedabad, India: Mapin Publishing Pvt. Ltd., 1991.

Oki, Morihiro. *India Fairs and Festivals.* Tokyo: Gakken Co. Ltd., 1989.

Saili, Ganesh, and Kamal Gill. *A Passage Through India.* New Delhi: Lustre Press Pvt. Ltd., 1994.

Singh, Khushwant. *India: An Introduction.* New Delhi: Vision Books Pvt. Ltd., 1990.

Srinivasan, Tadhika. *Cultures of the World: India.* Singapore: Times Books International, 1990.

Van Tulleken, Kit. *India.* Amsterdam: Time-Life Books, 1986.

On the Internet

Chef Sanjeev Kapoor
  http://www.sanjeevkapoor.com/

Incredible India
  http://www.incredibleindia.org/

Khana Khazana
  http://www.khanakhazana.com/

blanch—Process by which a shelled nut is placed in boiling water for one or two minutes, then cooled.

Bollywood (BALL-ee-wood)—The Hindi film industry in India.

cardamom (KAR-duh-mum)—The aromatic capsular fruit of an Indian herb of the ginger family. Its seeds are used as a spice or condiment and in medicine.

exile (EK-syl)—Absence from one's country or home, usually for political reasons.

garnish (GAR-nish)—To add decorative or savory touches to a food or drink.

ghee (GHEE)—A thin, clarified butter made especially in India.

gram flour—Flour made from ground chickpeas.

maida (MAY-daa)—Finely milled flour, like pastry flour.

marinate (MAYR-ih-nayt)—To soak meat or other ingredients in a sauce for a period of time before they are cooked.

monsoon (mon-SOON)—Heavy rain brought by seasonal winds.

Mughlai (MOOG-la-ee)—South Asian cuisine influenced by the imperial kitchens of the Mughal Empire.

palanquin (pal-un-KEEN)—A vehicle for carrying usually one passenger, consisting of a covered or boxlike platform carried by means of poles resting on the shoulders of several men.

pressure cooker (PREH-shur KOO-kur)—An airtight utensil used to quickly cook or preserve foods by means of high-temperature steam under pressure.

pulses (PUL-sez)—The edible seeds of various crops (such as peas, beans, or lentils) of the legume family.

saffron (SAA-fron)—The deep orange aromatic dried stigmas of a purple-flowered crocus used to color and flavor foods.

simmer—To cook gently in liquid below or just at the boiling point.

temper—To smooth out a flavor by mixing in or adding a usually liquid ingredient.

vegetarian (veh-jeh-TAYR-ee-un)—A person who does not eat meat and follows a plant-based diet including fruits, vegetables, cereal grains, nuts, and seeds, with or without dairy products and eggs.

Index

ABOUT THE
AUTHOR

Khadija Ejaz was born in Lucknow, India, and was raised in Muscat, Sultanate of Oman. She earned her bachelor's and master's degrees in Computer Science and Management Information Systems at the Oklahoma State University, Stillwater, and now lives between India, Oman, and Canada. A full-time IT professional, she freelances as a writer and has numerous writing credits to her name. Her other interests include filmmaking, acting, photography, volunteer work, and the theater. To learn more about Khadija, visit her website at http://khadijaejaz.netfirms.com.